My Best Friend

A Story about Friendship and Diversity

Written by Amy McDonough

This book belongs to:

____

Artwork inspiration for this story was influenced by the watercolor painting of our boys, by artist Julie Roy. Used with permission.

Friends come in different colors and sizes.
All of us are unique.

But my best friend is the BEST!
He can't be beat.

We are different than each other in many ways.

My eyes are golden brown.

His eyes are bright blue.

My hair is black and curly.

His hair is blonde and straight.

My skin is golden brown.

His skin is light and fair.

We both love trains!

We play all day!

He lives in a house.

I live in an apartment.

He lives with his mom and dad.

I live with my mom. I visit my dad.

He is an only child.

I have a grown-up brother and sister.

We both love going outside!

We play all day!

My favorite color is purple.

His favorite color is yellow.

I eat cheese sticks and sandwiches.

He eats cottage cheese and seaweed.

I like to build things.

He likes to destroy them.

We both play with
other friends sometimes.

But we always come back together.

Because we are BEST friends!!

More Stories from Rising Butterfly Press

Children grow, learn, and spread their wings through stories.

Discover more books written by Amy McDonough:

My Best Friend
 A heartfelt story celebrating friendship, kindness, and the joy
 of being yourself.

My First Day of Preschool
 A comforting adventure that helps little learners feel brave and
excited as they begin their preschool journey.

My Family Farm Field Trip
 A special trip to a family farm where children discover where food
comes from and why farmers are the real MVPs of the community.

More adventures coming soon!

Did you find the butterflies hiding in this book?